HOW DO AIRPLANES STAY UP?

by Debbie Vilardi

Cody Koala
An Imprint of Pop!
popbooksonline.com

abdobooks.com
Published by Pop!, a division of ABDO, PO Box 398166, Minneapolis, Minnesota 55439.

Printed in the United States of America, North Mankato, Minnesota

082018
012019
THIS BOOK CONTAINS RECYCLED MATERIALS

Cover Photo: iStockphoto
Interior Photos: iStockphoto, 1, 6, 18; Shutterstock Images, 5 (top), 5 (bottom left), 5 (bottom right), 9, 10–11, 13, 14, 16–17, 21

Editor: Meg Gaertner
Series Designer: Laura Mitchell

Library of Congress Control Number: 2018949242

Publisher's Cataloging-in-Publication Data
Names: Vilardi, Debbie, author.
Title: How do airplanes stay up? / by Debbie Vilardi.
Description: Minneapolis, Minnesota : Pop!, 2019 | Series: Science questions | Includes online resources and index.
Identifiers: ISBN 9781532162138 (lib. bdg.) | ISBN 9781641855846 (pbk) | ISBN 9781532163197 (ebook)
Subjects: LCSH: Planes (Airplanes)--Juvenile literature. | Aerodynamics--Juvenile literature. | Flying-machines--Juvenile literature. | Children's questions and answers--Juvenile literature.
Classification: DDC 500--dc23

Hello! My name is

Cody Koala

Pop open this book and you'll find QR codes like this one, loaded with information, so you can learn even more!

Scan this code* and others like it while you read, or visit the website below to make this book pop.

popbooksonline.com/airplanes-stay-up

*Scanning QR codes requires a web-enabled smart device with a QR code reader app and a camera.

Table of Contents

Chapter 1

Four Forces

People can fly even without wings. They ride in airplanes. They soar higher than most birds.

Watch a video here!

Airplanes fly by balancing four **forces**. These forces are **gravity**, lift, **drag**, and thrust. Together these forces keep an airplane up and moving forward.

The Wright brothers made the first flight on December 17, 1903. It lasted for 12 seconds.

Chapter 2

Overcoming Gravity

Gravity is a force that pulls things toward Earth. It is the reason things fall down. An airplane must overcome gravity to fly.

Complete an activity here!

Airplanes need an upward force that is stronger than gravity. This force is called lift. Lift has to do with **air pressure**.

Chapter 3

Achieving Lift

Air moves from places of high air pressure to places of low pressure. Airplane wings are designed so the air pressure is lower above the wing.

Learn more here!

The top of the wing is curved. The bottom is flat. This increases the air pressure under the wing. The air pushes up on the wing. Lift happens. The airplane flies.

The shape of an airplane wing is called an airfoil.

Chapter 4

Drag and Thrust

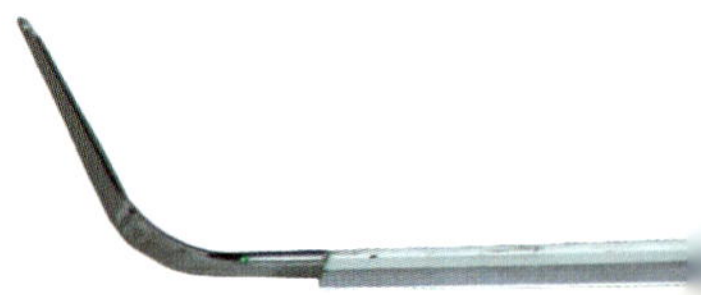

Air pushes against an airplane as it flies. This is the force of drag. Drag holds the airplane back. Airplanes need a forward force stronger than drag.

Learn more here!

Airplanes have engines that burn fuel. These engines give airplanes thrust.

This force pushes the airplane forward. If thrust is stronger than drag, the airplane will move.

Airplanes overcome gravity with lift. They overcome drag with thrust. By using these forces, humans achieve flight.

Even paper airplanes balance the forces of gravity, lift, thrust, and drag.

The Four Forces of Flight

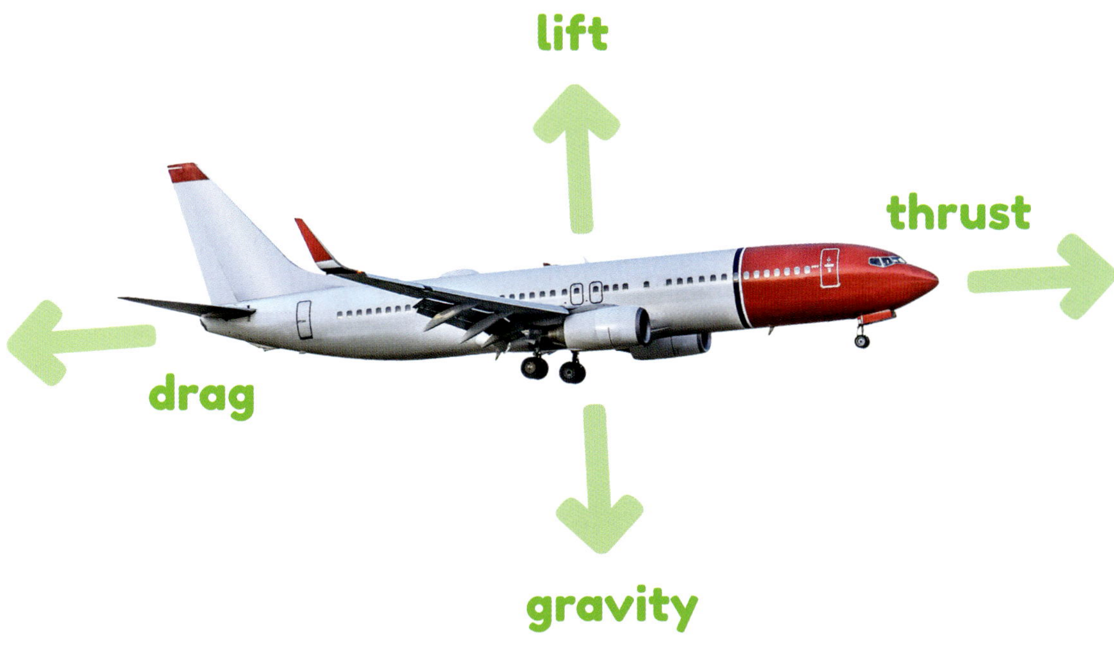

Making Connections

Text-to-Self

Have you ever been in an airplane? If yes, how did you like it? If no, would you want to ride in an airplane? Where would you want to go?

Text-to-Text

Have you read other books about airplanes? What new information did you learn?

Text-to-World

You learned about how airplanes move. How does this compare to how other vehicles move?

Glossary

air pressure – the force of air on an object.

drag – a force that slows the movement of an object when it moves through a liquid or a gas.

force – something that changes the movement of an object.

gravity – a force that pulls objects toward Earth.

Index

Online Resources

popbooksonline.com

Thanks for reading this Cody Koala book!

Scan this code* and others like it in this book, or visit the website below to make this book pop!

popbooksonline.com/airplanes-stay-up

*Scanning QR codes requires a web-enabled smart device with a QR code reader app and a camera.